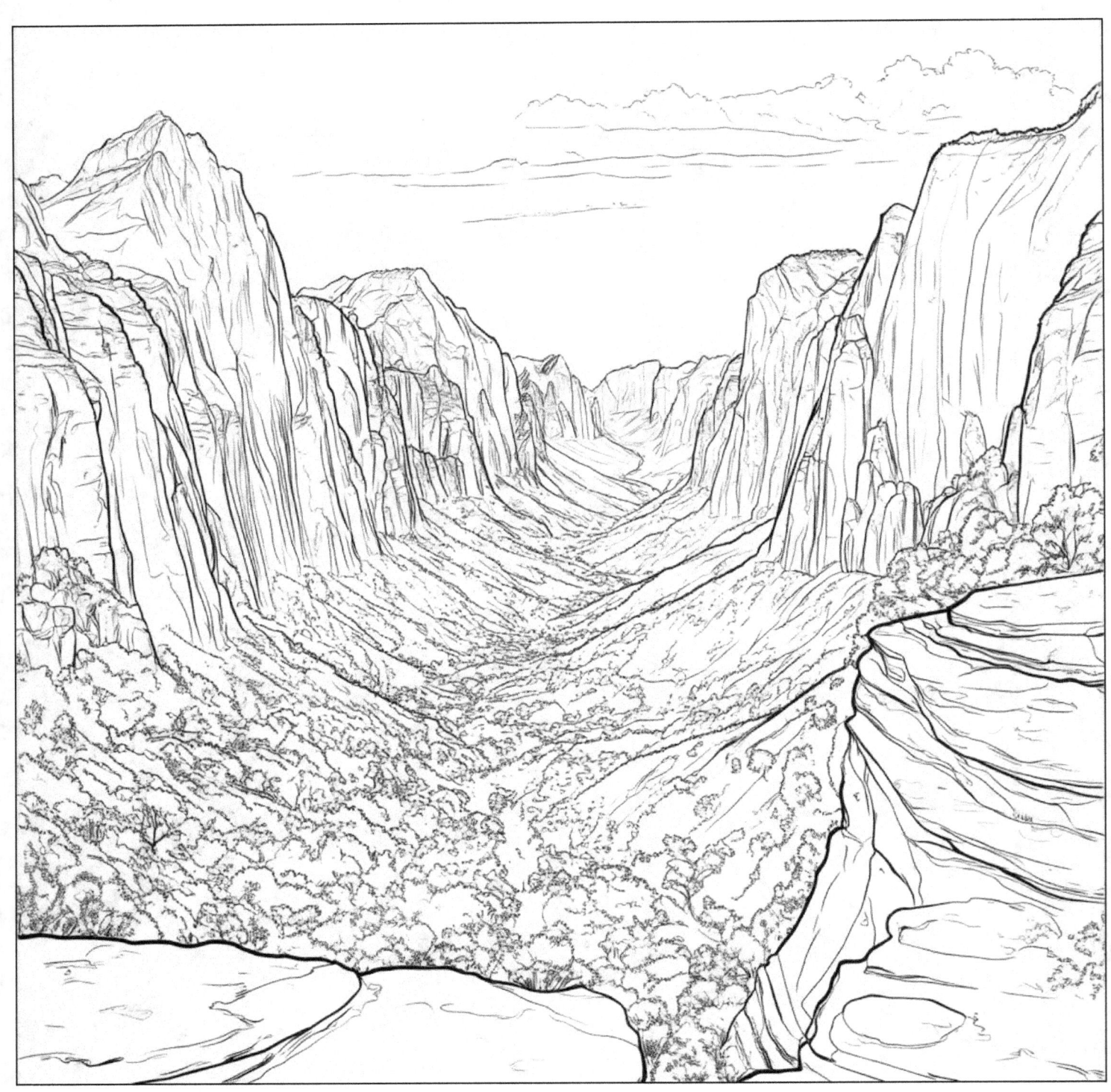

Angel's Landing, Utah

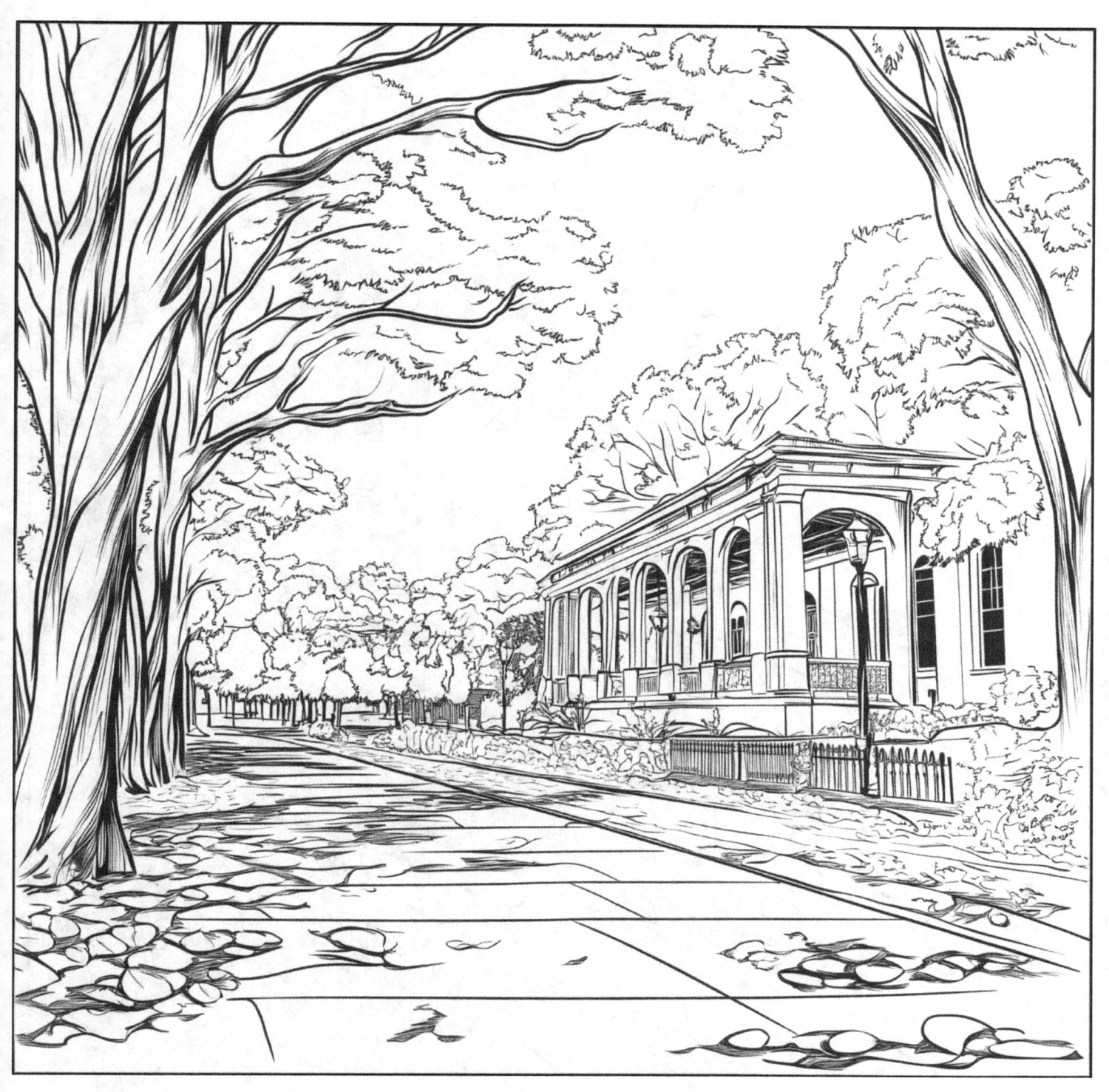

Bathhouse Row, Arkansas

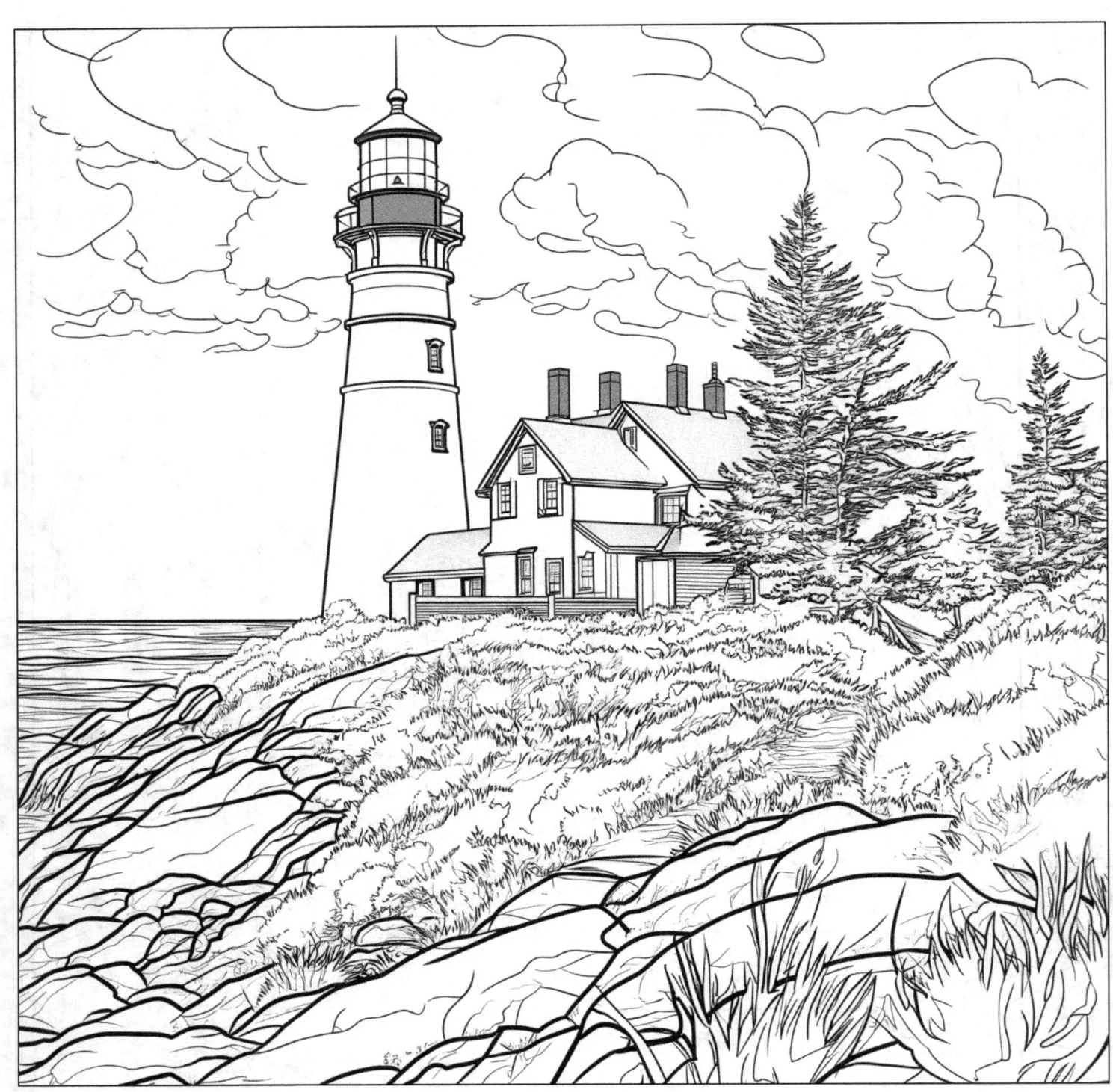

Cape Elizabeth, Maine

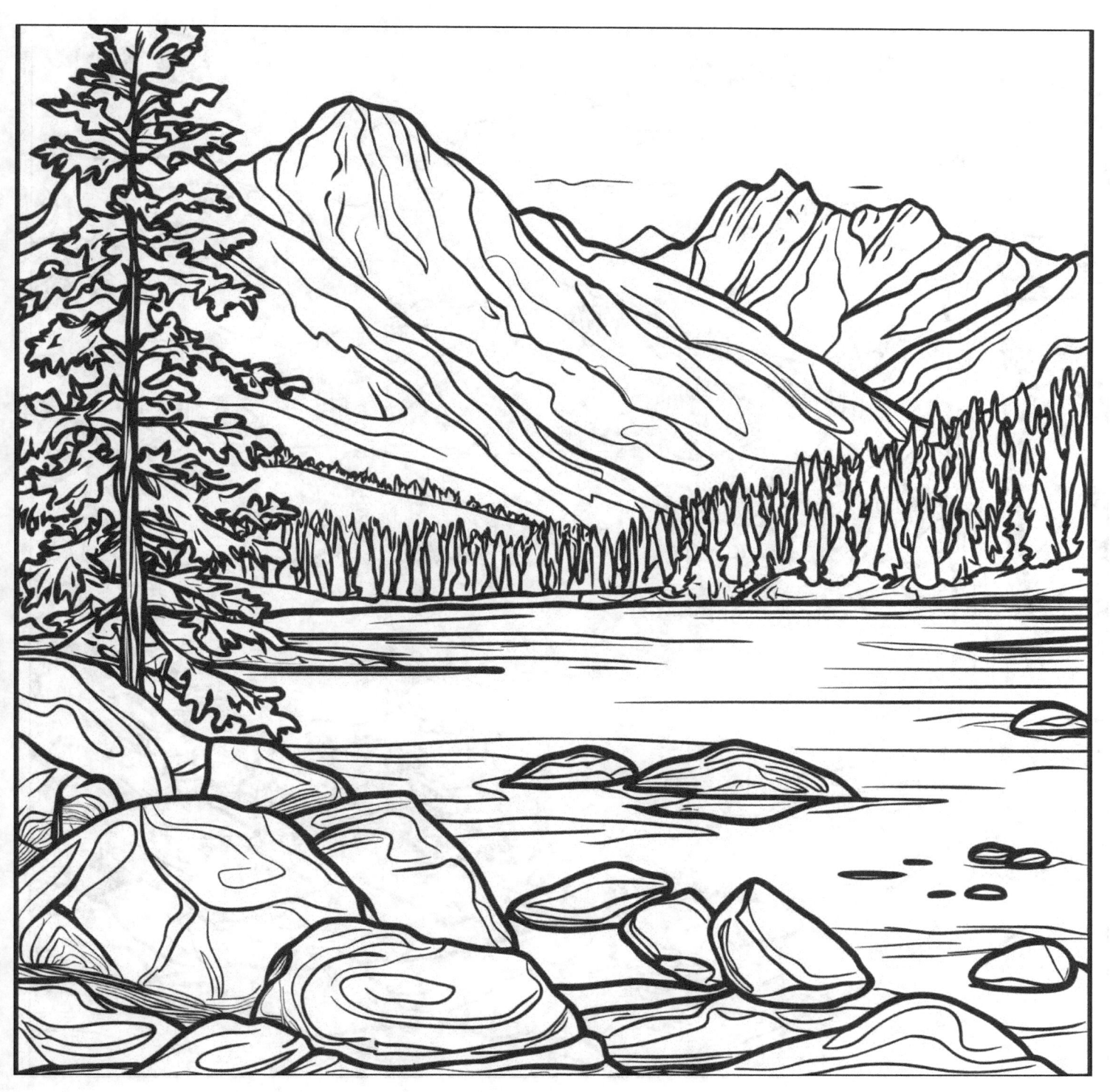

Bear Lake, Colorado

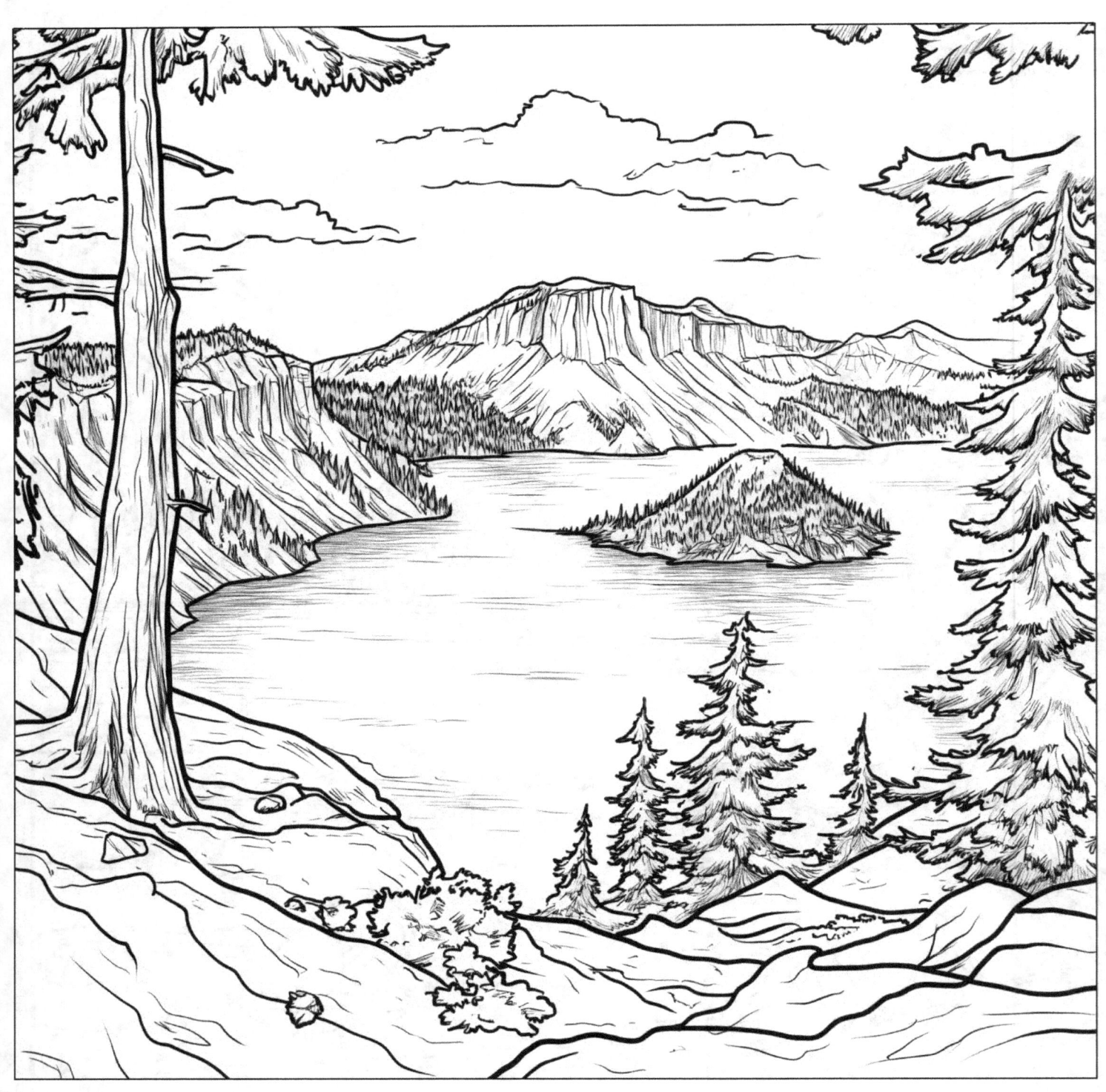

Crater Lake, Oregon

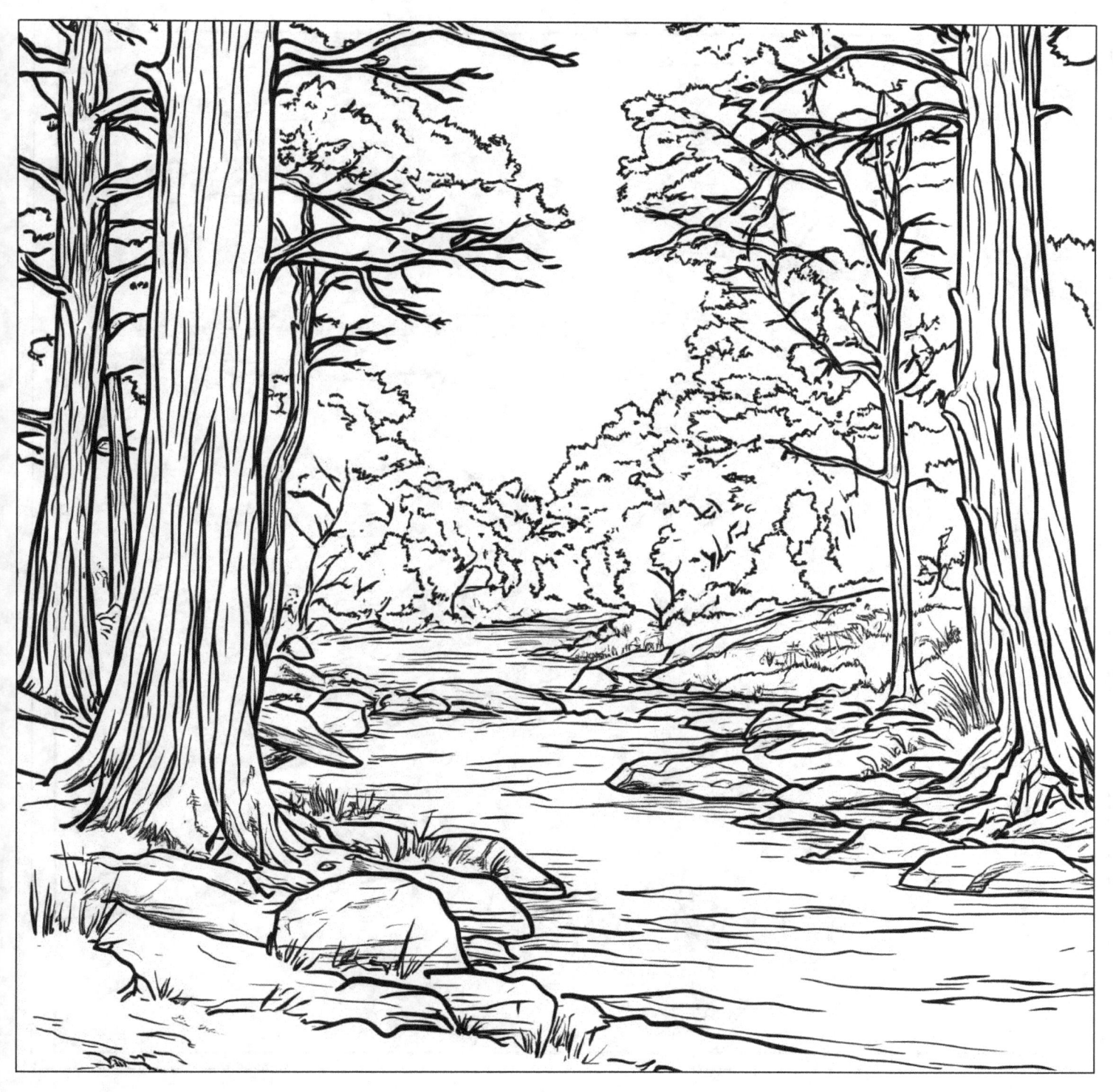

Cibolo Creek, Boerne TX

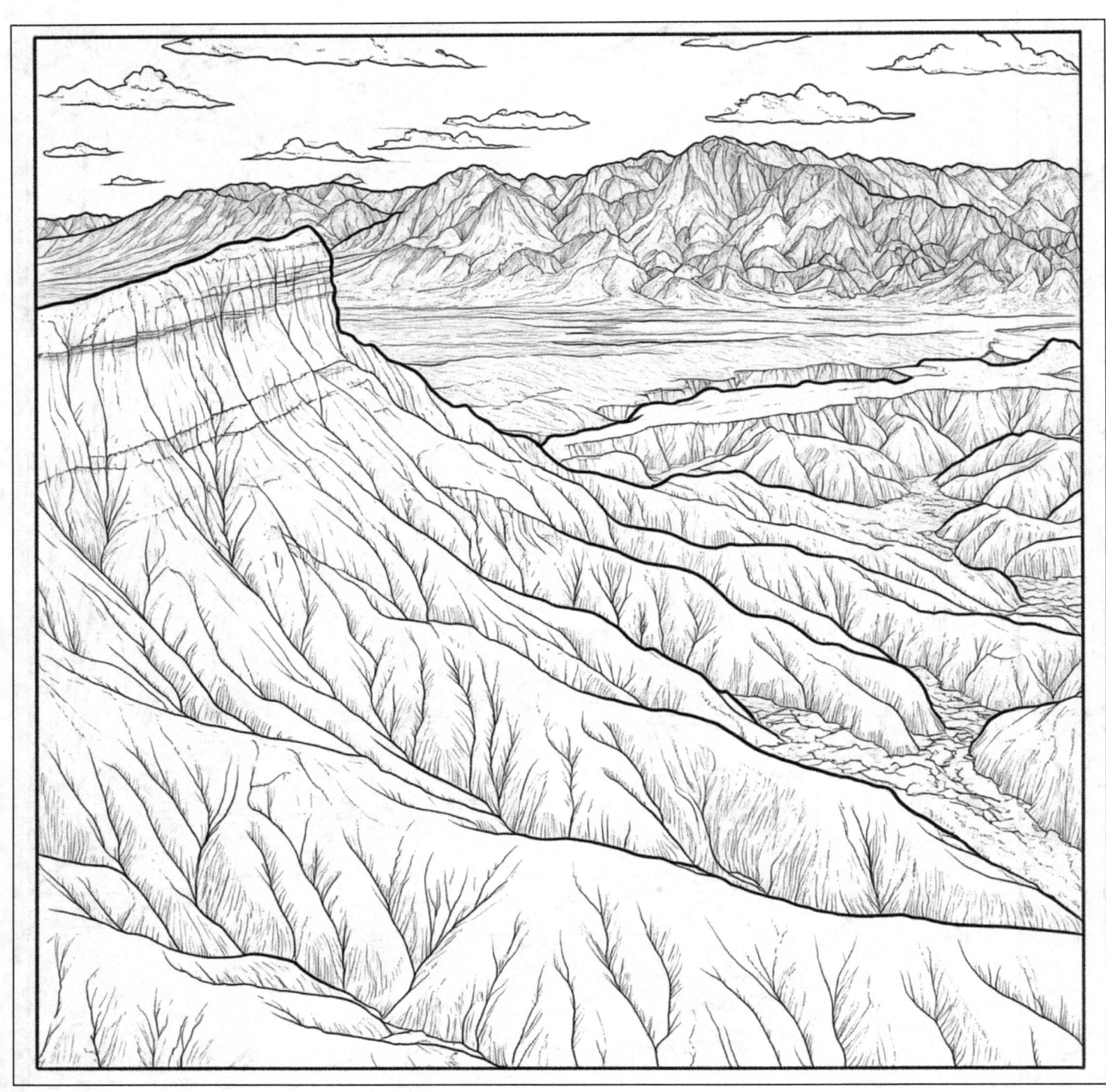

Zabriskie Point, California

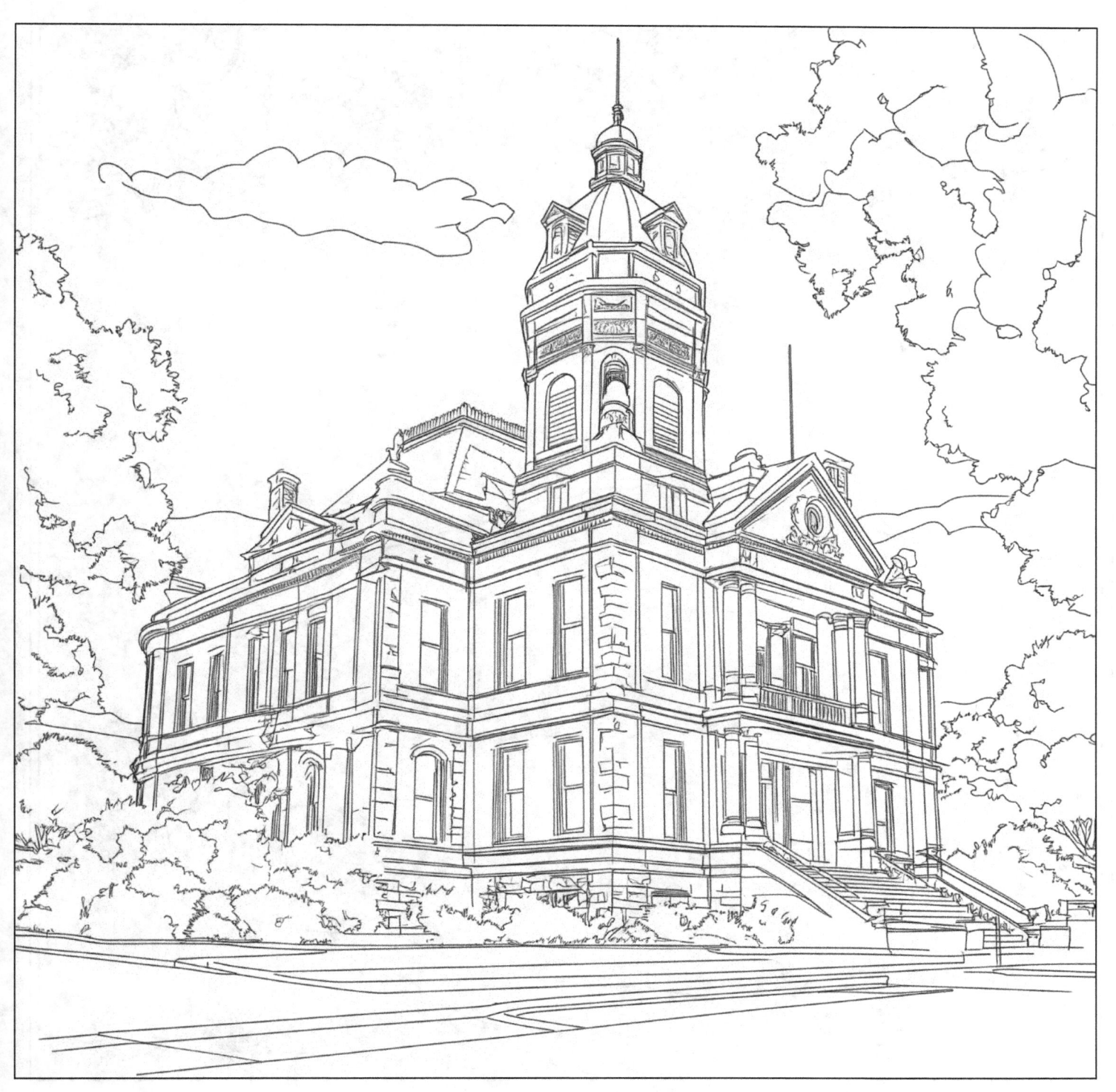

Denton County Courthouse, Denton TX

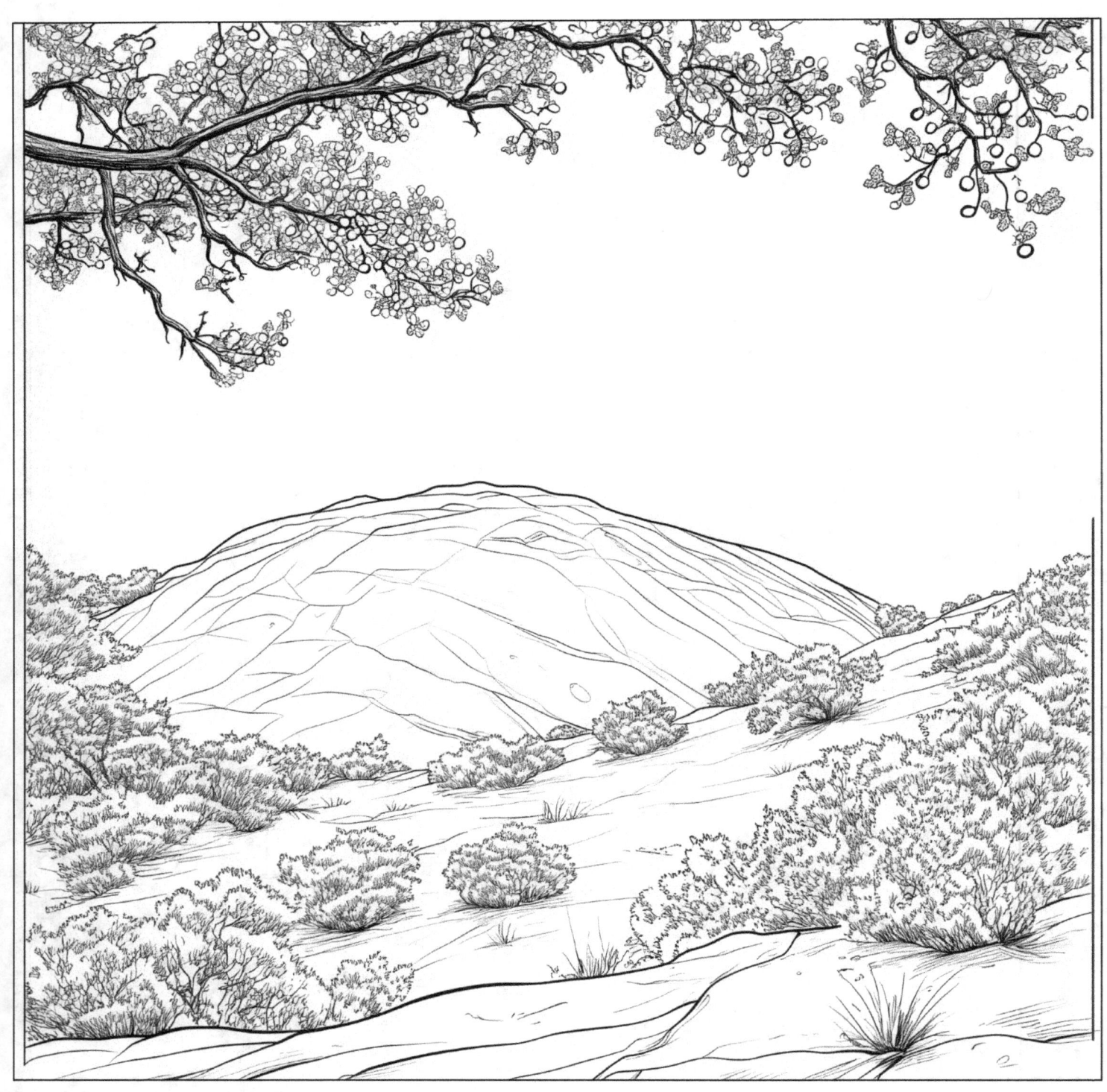

Enchanted Rock, TX

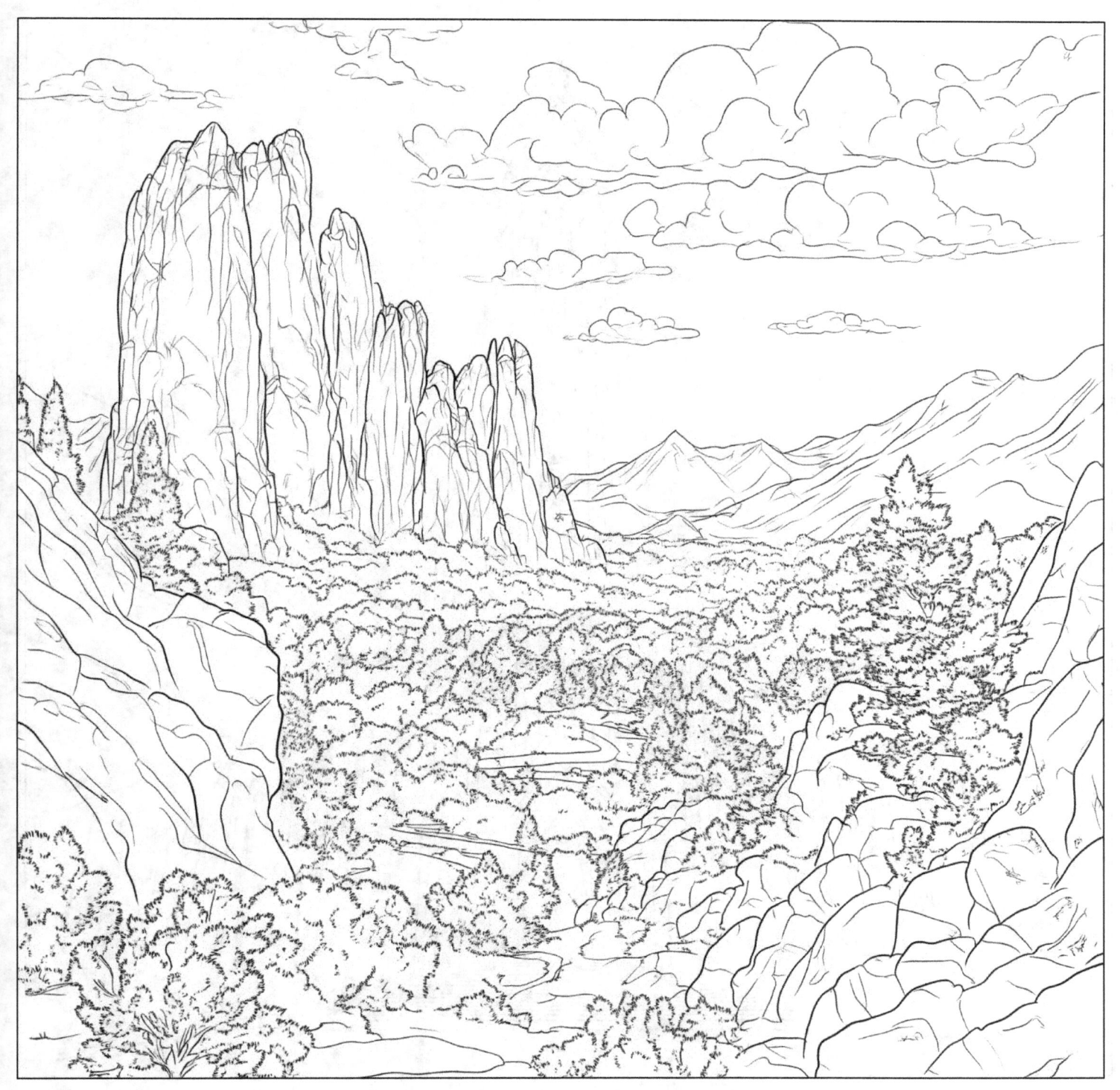

Garden of the Gods, Colorado

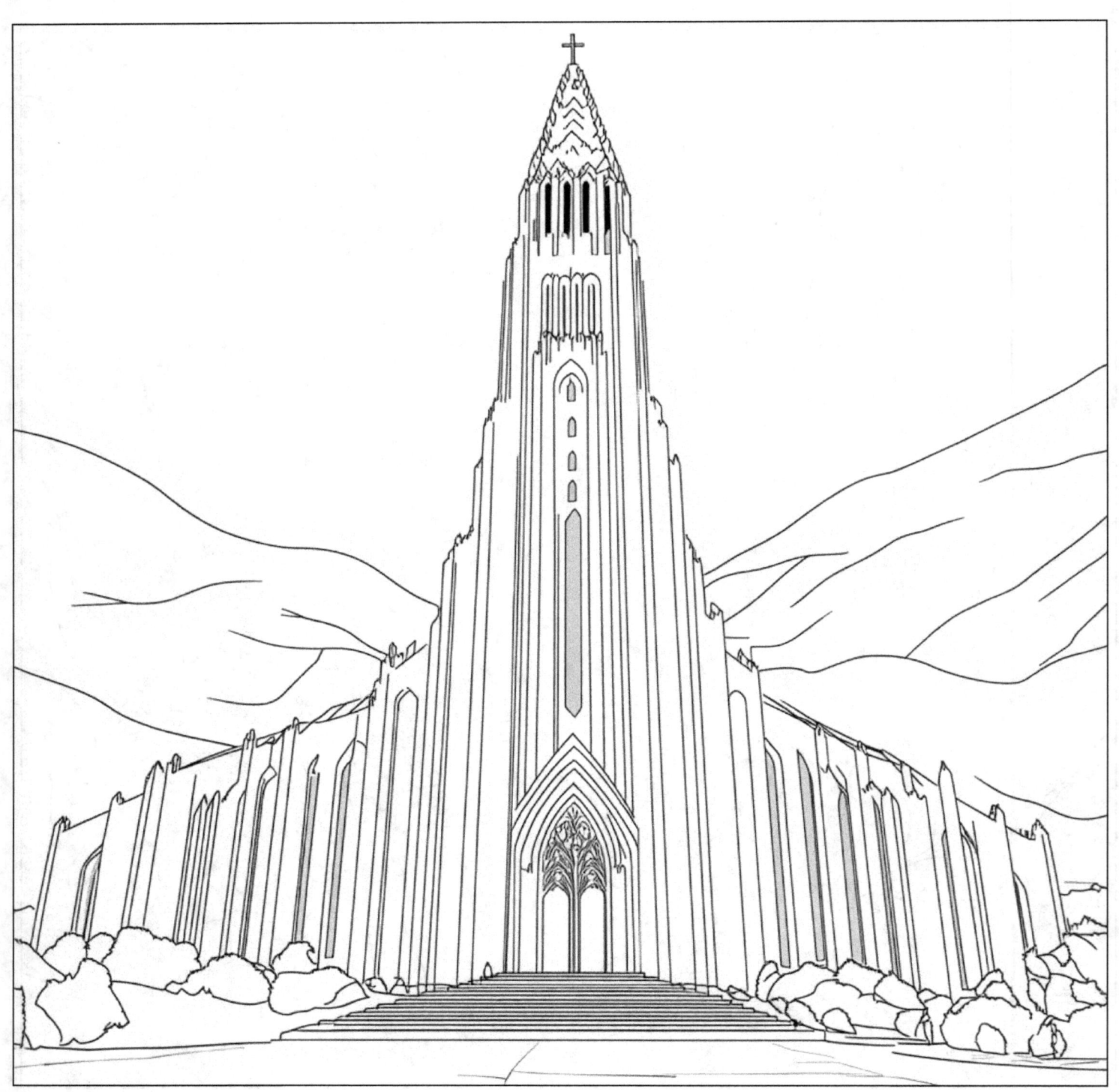

Hallgrimskirkja, Iceland

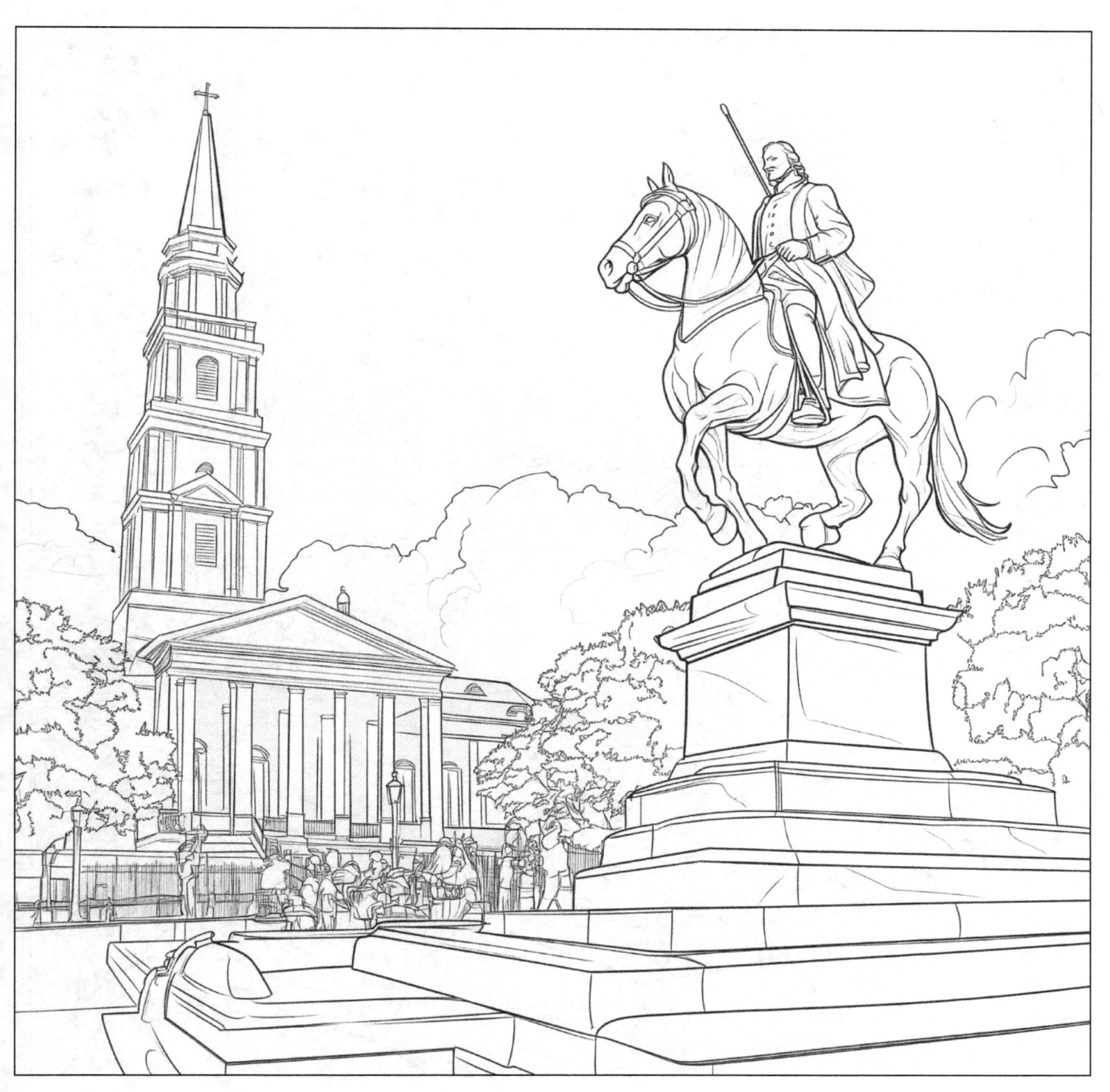

Jackson Square, Louisiana

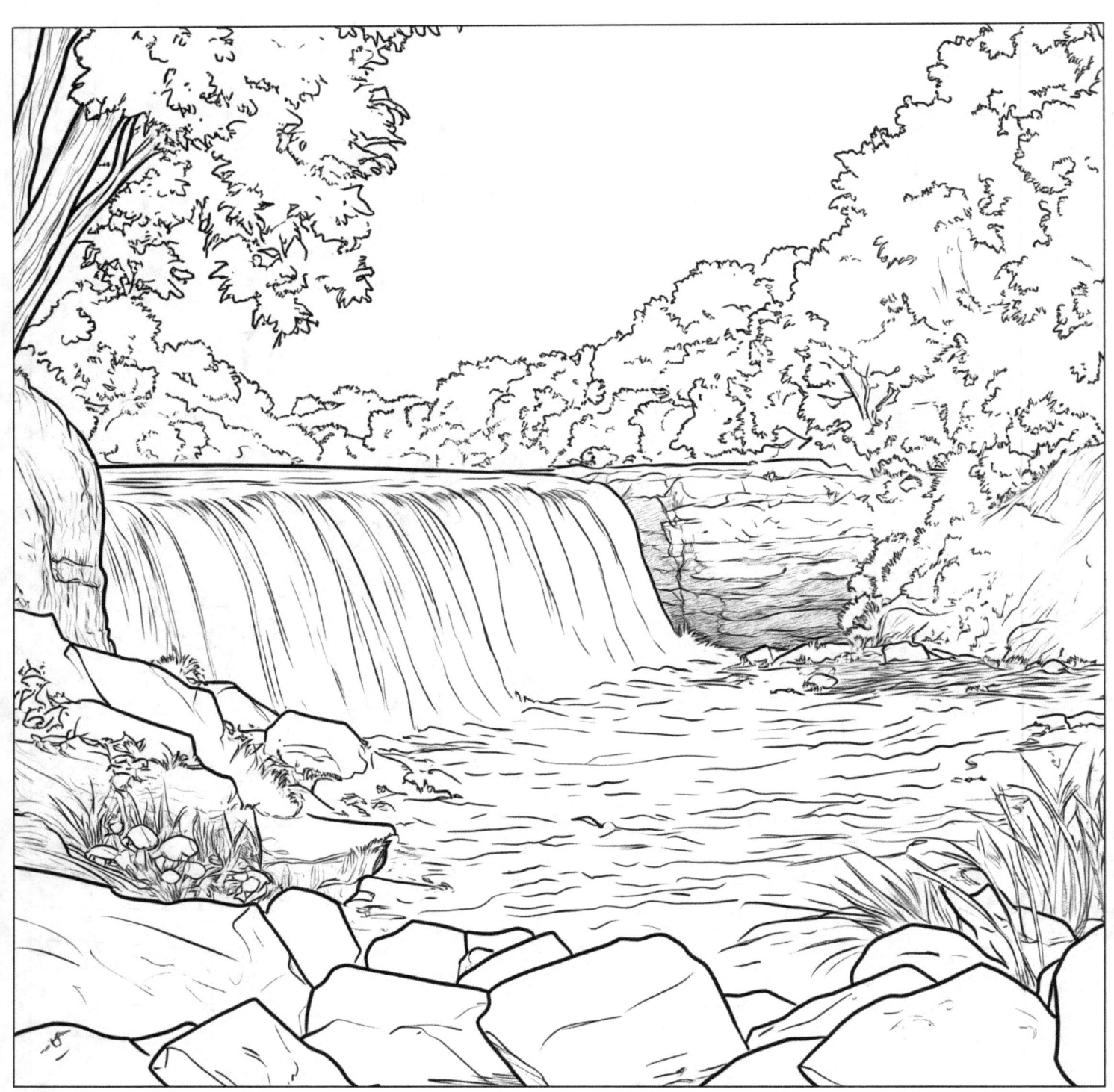

Little Niagara, Oklahoma

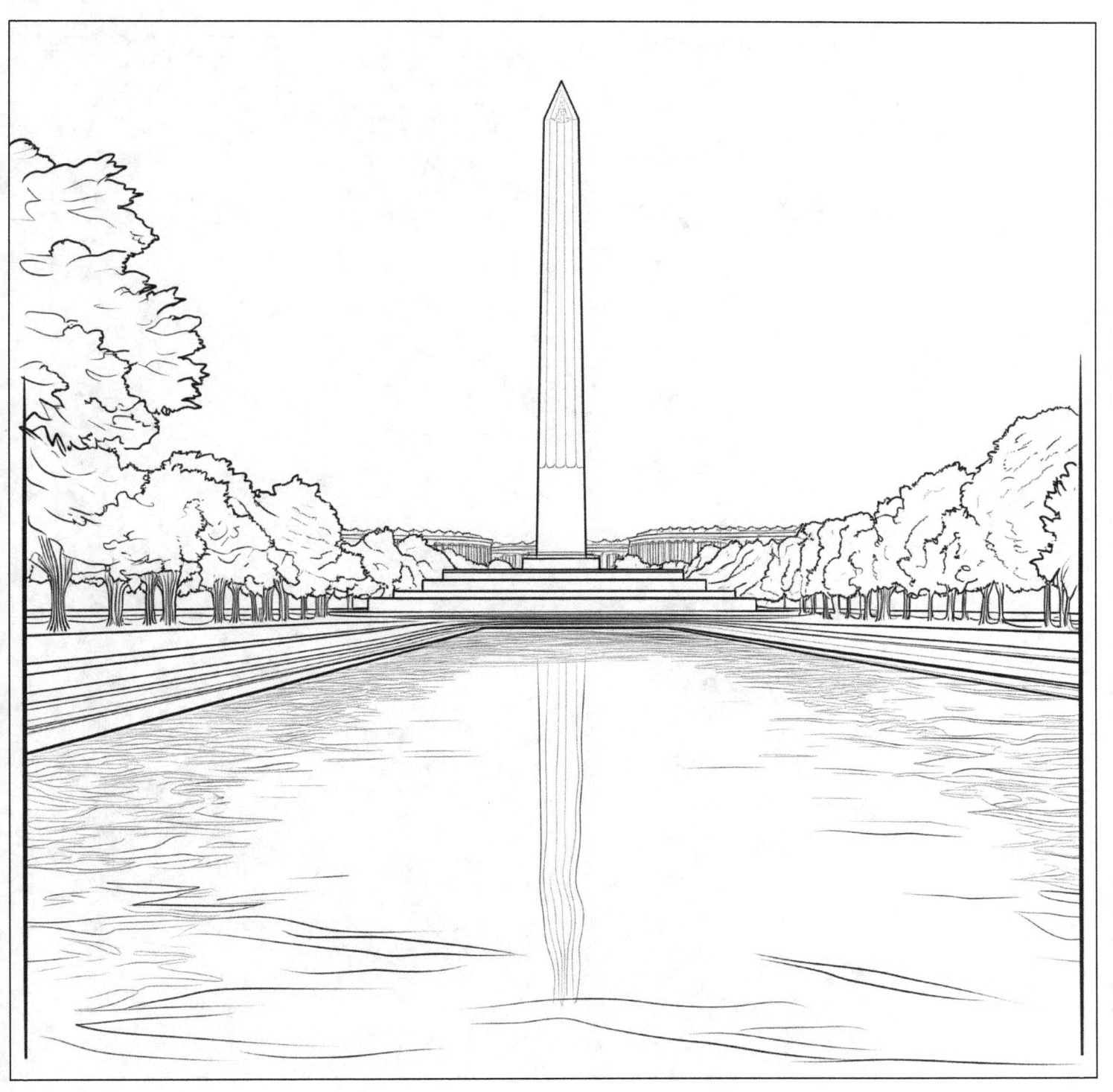

National Mall, Washington DC

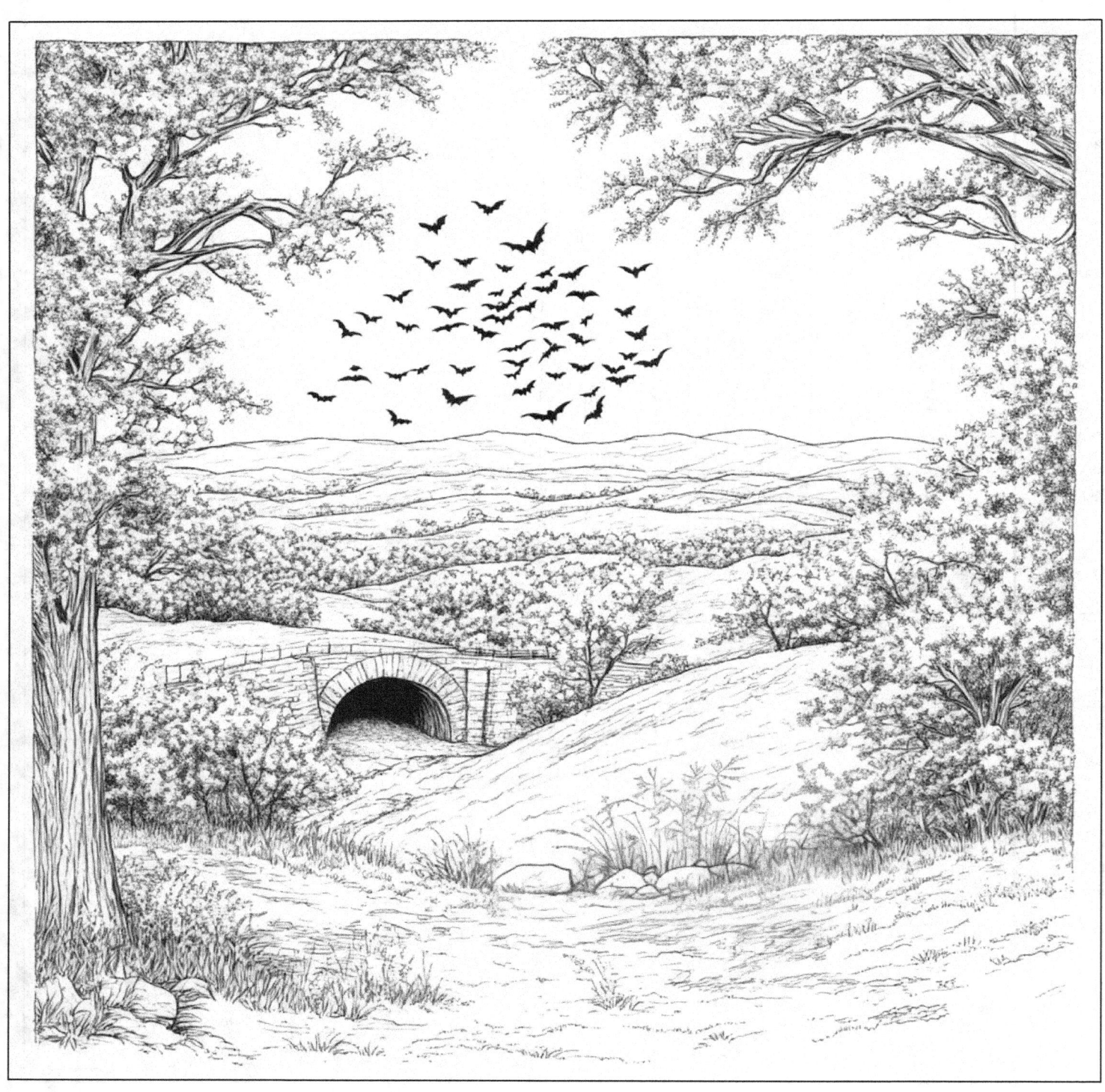

Old Tunnel State Park, Texas

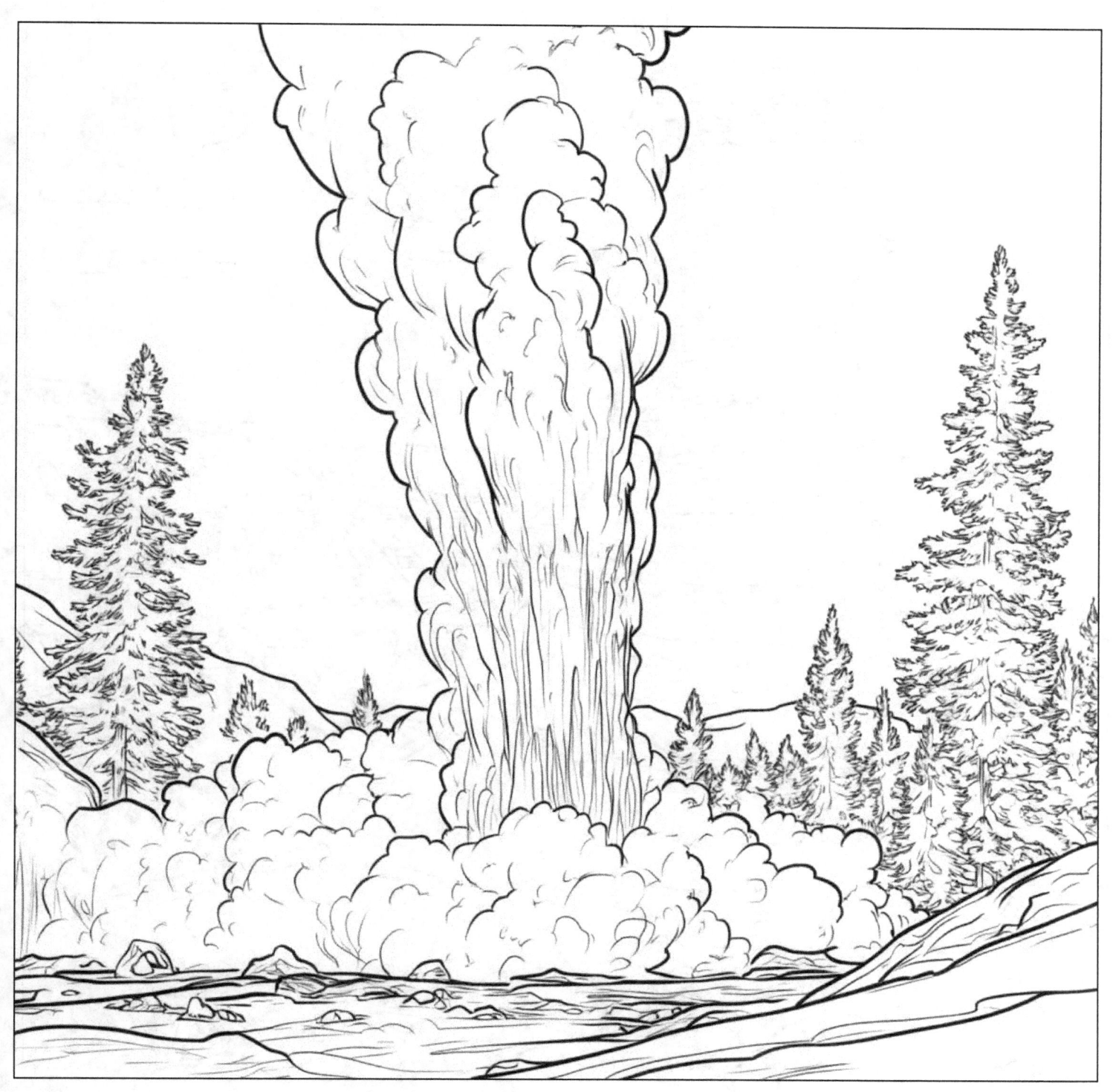

Old Faithful Geyser, Wyoming

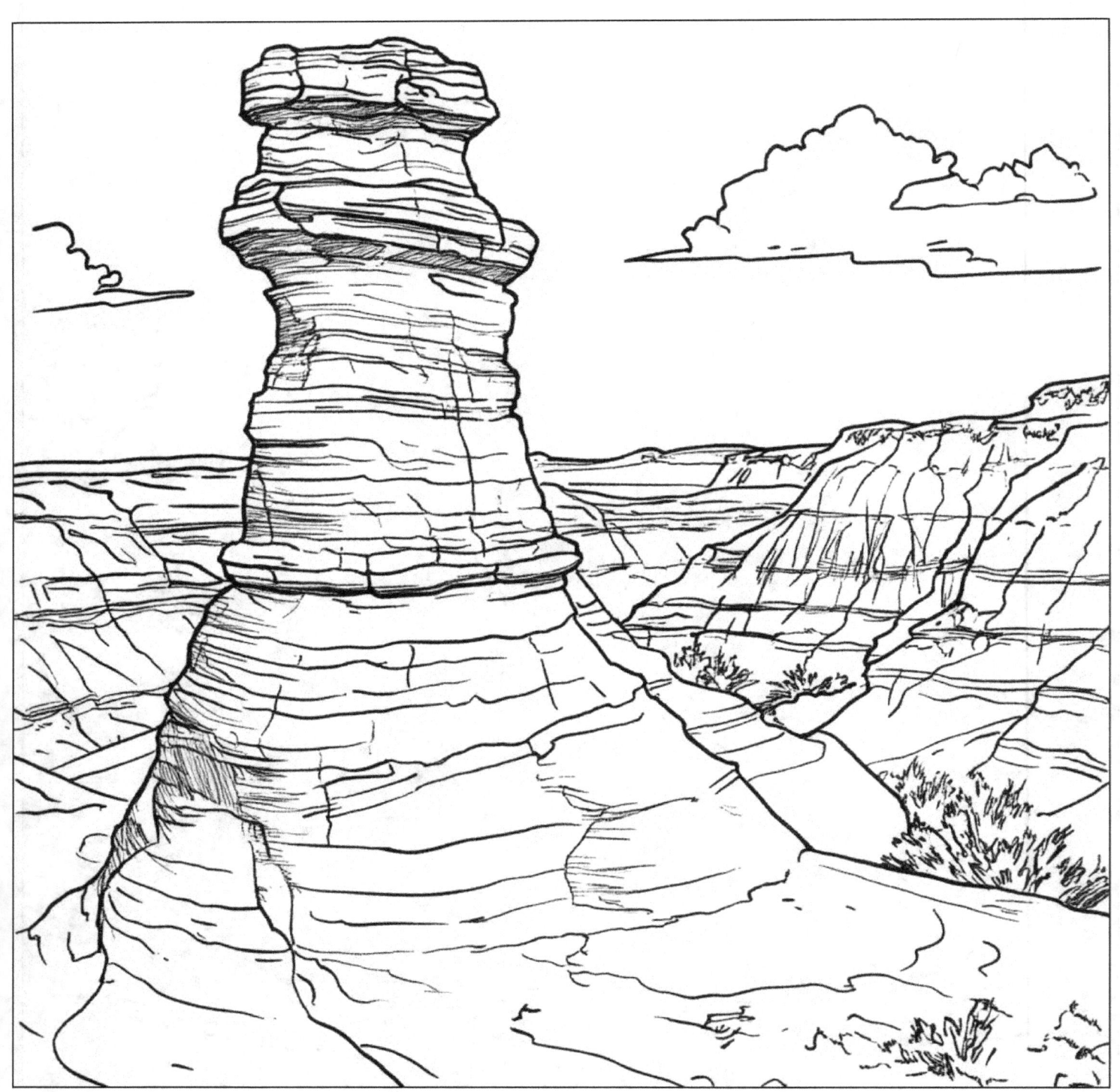

The Lighthouse, Palo Duro State Park, Texas

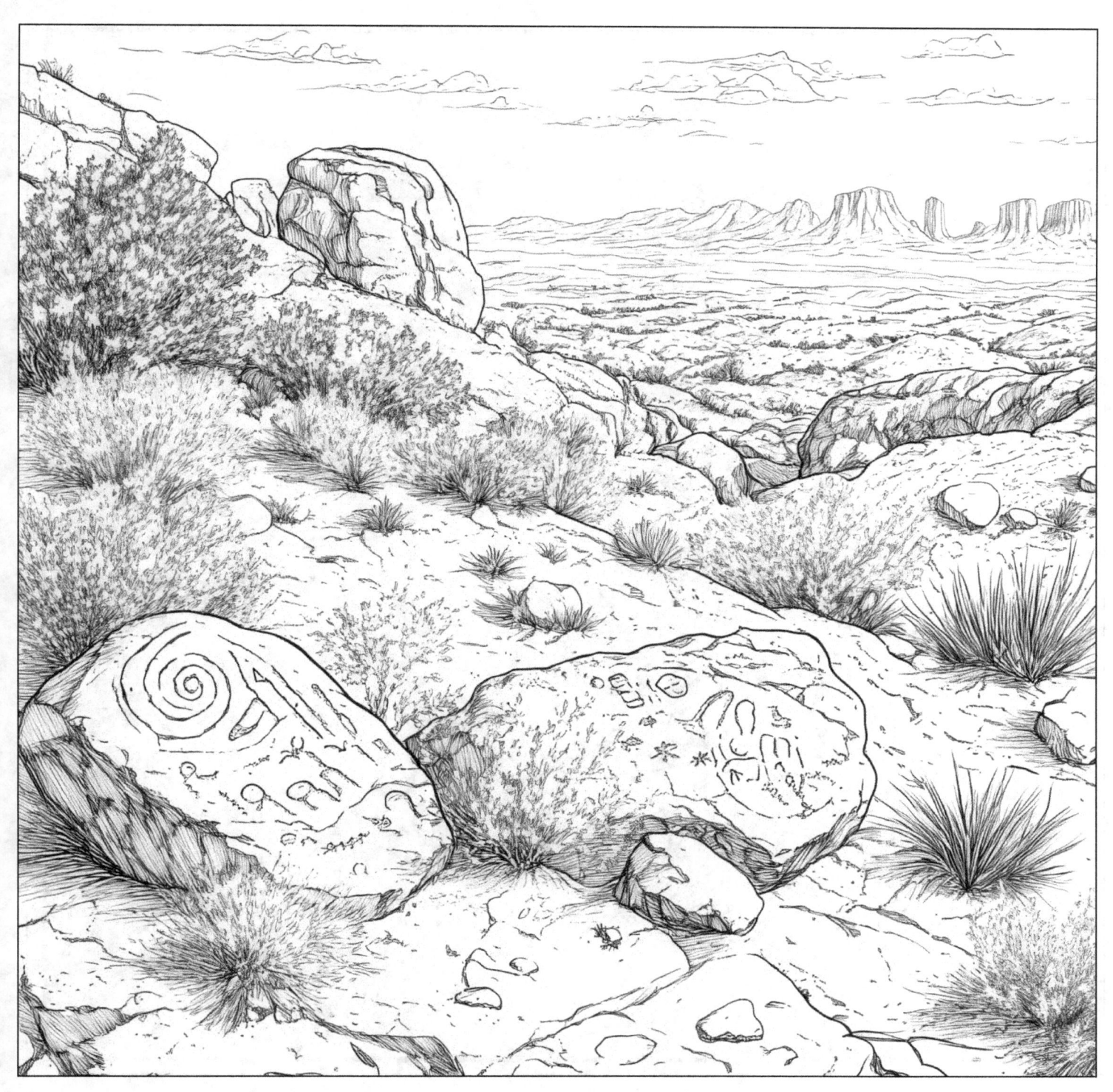

Petroglyph National Monument, New Mexico

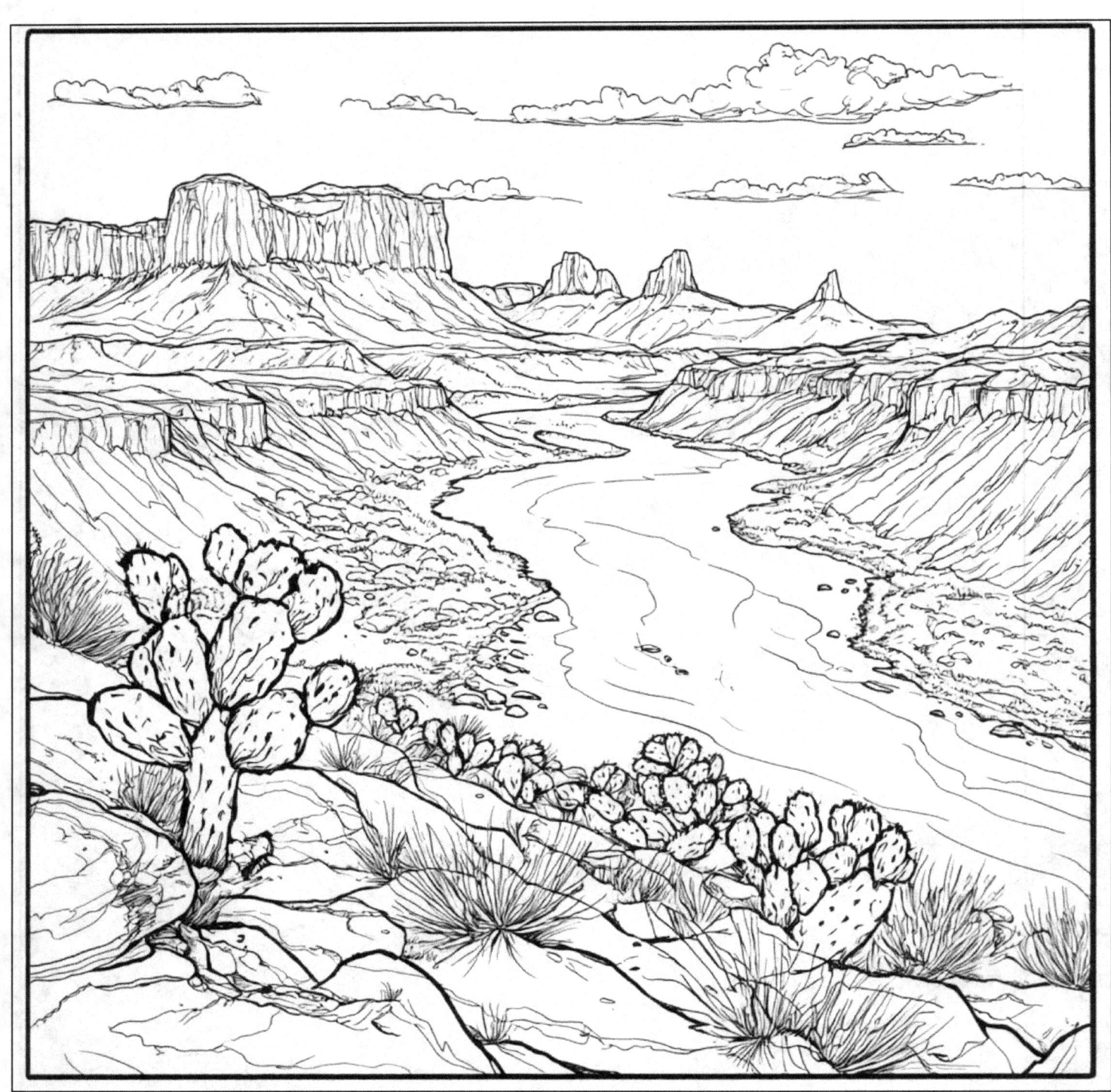

Rio Grande River, Big Bend National Park, Texas

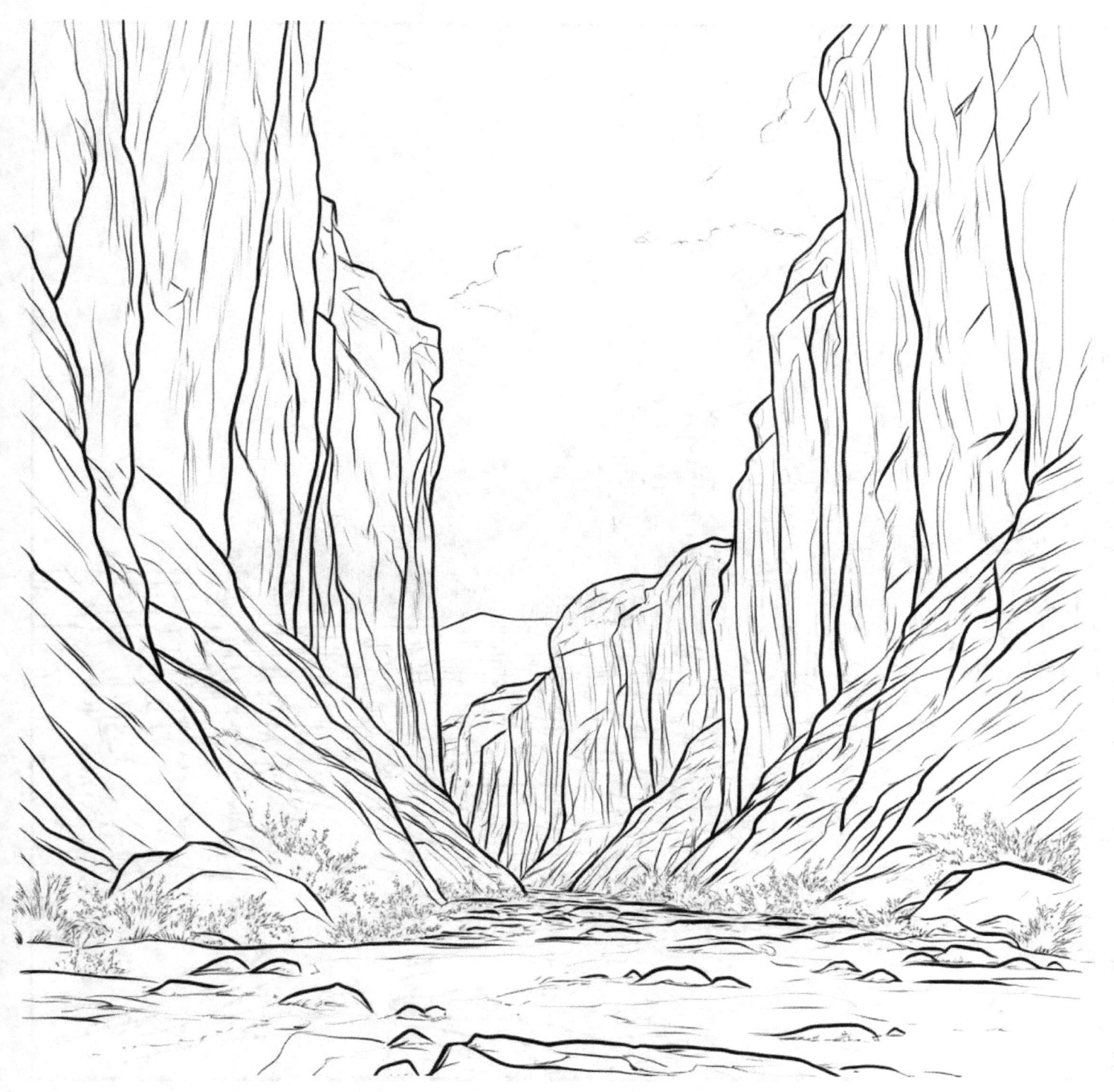

Santa Elena Canyon, Big Bend National Park, Texas

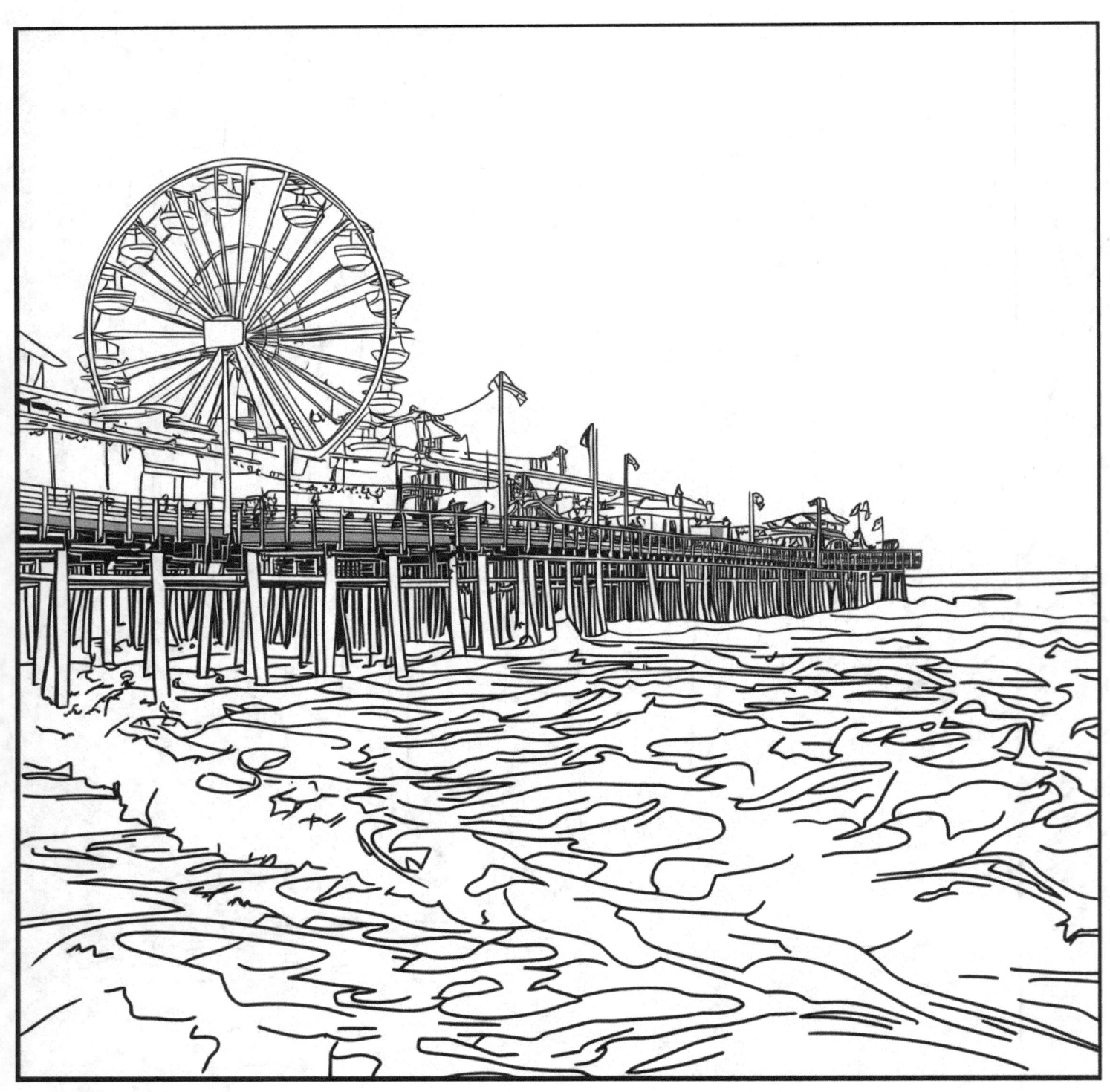

Santa Monica Pier, California

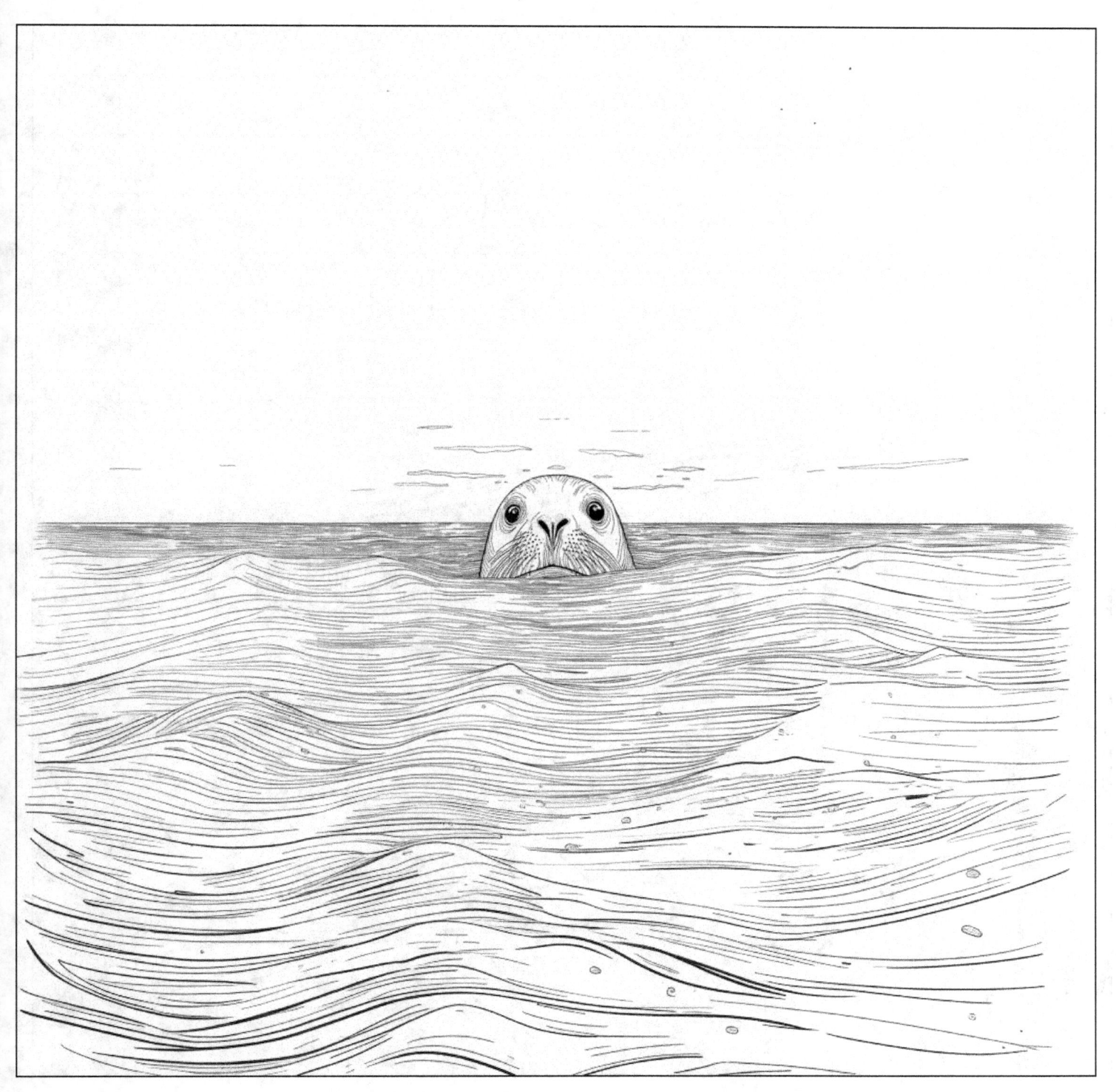

Plymouth Beach, Massachusetts

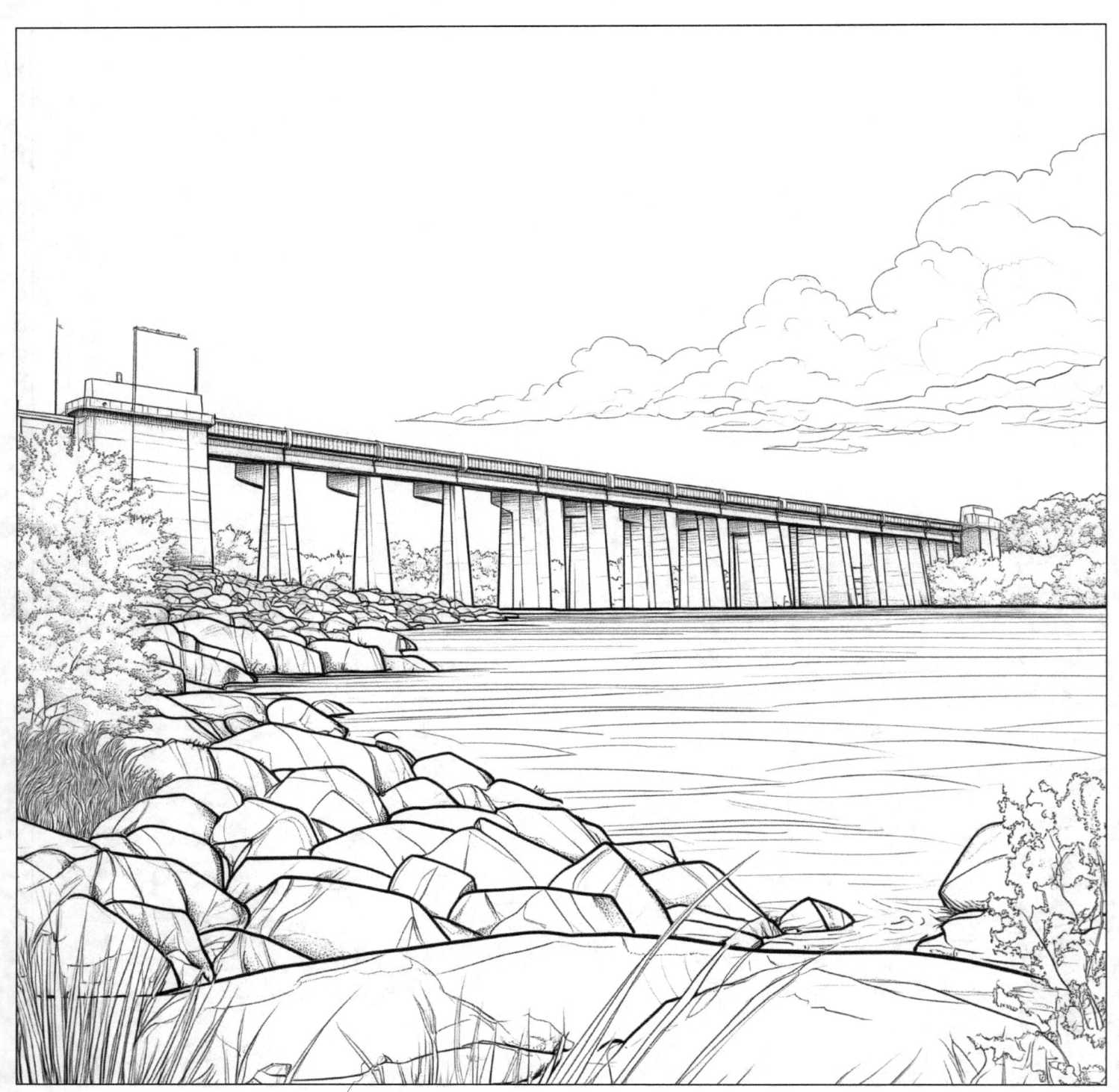

The Big Dam Bridge, Arkansas